Living

Jean Chapman

Rosen Classroom Books & Materials™
New York

Living things need food, water, air, and a place to stay safe.

Plants are living things. Plants make their own food with sunlight, water, and gases from the air.

Animals are living things. Some animals fly. Others walk on land or live in the water.

People are living things. People can run, jump, and dance.

People and animals give **birth** to babies that look like them. Their bodies **grow** and **change**.

A plant grows from a seed.

An apple seed grows into an apple tree.

Some things are not **alive**. A bike is not a living thing. It cannot grow like a plant, a person, or an animal.

A table is not a living thing. It cannot eat, drink, or move like people can.

A doll is not a living thing. It
cannot swim, talk, or read a book
like people can.

Can you find the living things in this picture? Can you find some things that are not alive?

Glossary

alive   Having life, like a plant, animal, or person.

birth   The act of coming into life.

change   To become different.

grow   To get bigger.